SUNSHINE

Brightens Springtime

by
Charles Ghigna

illustrated by
Laura Watson

PICTURE WINDOW BOOKS
a capstone imprint

Sunshine spreads across the lake.

2

Sunshine warms us when we wake.

Sunshine finds a bunny's home.

Sunshine heats an ice-cream cone!

5

Sunshine melts away the snow.

Sunshine helps the garden grow.

Sunshine makes a shadow-flower.

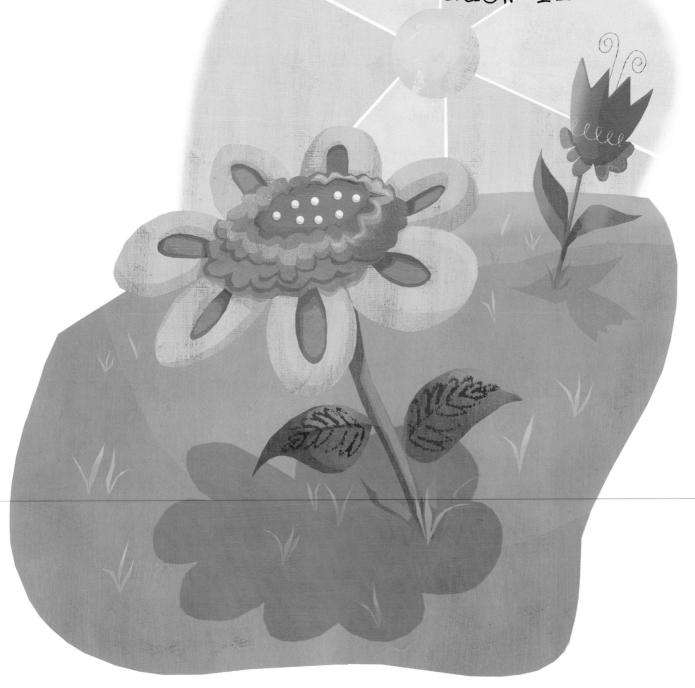

Sunshine shadows grow each hour.

Sunshine beams through rows of trees.

Sunshine sparkles on the leaves.

Sunshine glimmers on the grain.

Sunshine gleams upon the pane.

Sunshine hides behind the clouds.

Sunshine brightens up the crowd.

Sunshine follows April showers.

Sunshine dries the rain-soaked flowers.

17

Sunshine warms each afternoon.

Sunshine glows upon the moon.

Sunshine brings new life each spring.

Sunshine shines on everything!

All About Sunshine

- Sunlight comes from the sun. It takes just over 8 minutes for sunlight to travel from the sun to Earth.
- Earth would not have any plants without sunshine. Plant leaves soak up sunlight. Then the leaves turn the sunlight into energy for the plant. This process is called photosynthesis. Take a look at photosynthesis:

- Sunlight gives light and heat to Earth. Without it, Earth would be a cold, dark place.
- Too much sunlight can be bad for people's skin. But not getting enough sunlight can also cause health problems.

All the Titles in This Set:

Hail to Spring!
Raindrops Fall All Around
Sunshine Brightens Springtime
A Windy Day in Spring

Internet Sites

FactHound offers a safe, fun way to find Internet sites related to this book. All of the sites on FactHound have been researched by our staff.

Here's all you do:

Visit *www.facthound.com*

Type in this code: 9781479560318

Check out projects, games and lots more at
www.capstonekids.com

Super-cool stuff!

For Charlotte and Christopher.

Thanks to our adviser for his expertise, research, and advice:
Terry Flaherty, PhD, Professor of English
Minnesota State University, Mankato

Editors: Shelly Lyons and Elizabeth R. Johnson
Designer: Lori Bye
Art Director: Nathan Gassman
Production Specialist: Tori Abraham

The illustrations in this book were created with acrylics and digital collage.

Picture Window Books are published by Capstone,
1710 Roe Crest Drive, North Mankato, Minnesota 56003
www.capstonepub.com

Library of Congress Cataloging-in-Publication Data
Ghigna, Charles, author.
Sunshine brightens springtime / by Charles Ghigna ; illustrated by Laura Watson.
pages cm. — (Nonfiction picture books. Springtime weather wonders)
   Summary: "Introduces sunshine through fun, poetic text and colorful illustrations"—Provided by publisher.
   Audience: Ages 5-7.
   Audience: K to grade 3.
ISBN 978-1-4795-6031-8 (library binding : alk. paper)
ISBN 978-1-4795-6035-6 (big book)
ISBN 978-1-4795-6039-4 (ebook pdf)
ISBN 978-1-4795-6043-1 (board book)
1. Spring—Juvenile literature. 2. Sunshine—Juvenile literature. 3. Weather—Juvenile literature.
I. Watson, Laura, 1968- illustrator. II. Title.

Design Element
Shutterstock: Hans-Joerg Nisch

QB637.5.G485 2015
508.2—dc23   2014029002

Printed in Canada.
092014   008478FRS15